VOCABULARY 4

FOR YOUNG CATHOLICS

WRITTEN BY
SETON STAFF

SETON PRESS
FRONT ROYAL, VA

Executive Editor: Dr. Mary Kay Clark
Editors: Seton Staff
Illustrator: Benjamin Hatke

Seton Press
1350 Progress Drive
Front Royal, VA 22630
540-636-9990

For more information, visit us on the web at http://www.setonpress.com.
Contact us by e-mail at info@setonpress.com.

ISBN: 978-1-60704-126-9

Cover: *The Finding in the Temple,* Anonymous 19th Century German Artist

DEDICATED TO THE SACRED HEART OF JESUS

VOCABULARY 4 FOR YOUNG CATHOLICS

CONTENTS

NOTES FOR PARENTS

Preface

It is important for students to learn new words as well as different meanings of words they already know. It is also important for students to remember the new vocabulary words and definitions and to apply them in their speaking and writing. In this grade level, students are writing answers to specific questions as well as writing sentences in their other courses. The vocabulary words studied in this book will enhance those assignments.

Besides learning new words, or different meanings for words, students need to practice using words so they remember them over time. Repetition helps memorization. You will notice we have several exercises: looking up the words in a dictionary, comparing similar words and contrasting opposite words, using words in sentences, identifying words for a crossword puzzle, and an optional exercise using the thesaurus to find synonyms and antonyms. Seton sells the *Merriam-Webster's Intermediate Thesaurus*.

We believe students will become familiar with these words and comfortable enough with the words to use them in their speech and writing. Seton encourages you, the parent, to use these words in daily conversation, especially during the week your student is studying these words.

Notice that sometimes we use a word, such as an adjective, but the main entry in the dictionary will be a noun. In most cases, the adjective is included in the dictionary citation under the noun form of the word.

Lesson Contents

Exercise A: This is a list of vocabulary words and their part of speech. Students learn to look up words in the dictionary, to pronounce them correctly, and to locate the definition which is appropriate for the particular parts of speech.

Exercise B: These are sentences that require students to remember and to apply the words they have learned in the lesson. Many of these sentences are related to the Catholic Faith or Catholic life, following the directives of the Vatican regarding Catholic schools and textbooks used in Catholic schools.

Exercise C: Students need to apply their understanding of the words to more descriptive definitions.

Exercise D: These are word groups that further comprehension. The student must think about each word's meaning and match the two words that have either similar meanings or opposite meanings.

An optional thesaurus exercise is also suggested. As the student uses a thesaurus, he further expands his vocabulary as he learns synonyms and antonyms for the lesson's vocabulary words.

Crossword Puzzle: This is a popular exercise with students. This exercise is an enjoyable and rewarding way to recall the words they have used.

Suggested Procedure

Notice that there are six lessons per quarter. A quarter review test may be given at any time during the seventh, eighth, or ninth week of the quarter. Seton's lesson plans include a quarter review test.

We encourage parents to give a weekly quiz, the parent giving the definition and asking the student to write out the correct vocabulary word. Seton's lesson plans include weekly quizzes.

Each lesson may be completed within one week. It is up to the parent to determine whether the student should cover the exercises in three, four, or five days. Keep in mind that review, repetition, and application over several days helps the definitions to be more easily retained in the memory.

Approach 1: Complete one lesson in a week. During the week, complete Exercises A through D and the Crossword Puzzle. At the end of the week, the student takes a weekly quiz administered and graded by the parent.

Approach 2: Complete one lesson in a week. Complete the Crossword Puzzle. Students love crossword puzzles. However, students should not copy the definitions for the puzzle in writing the definitions for Exercise A, primarily because students need to practice using the dictionary. During the remainder of the week, complete Exercises A through D. At the end of the week, the student takes a weekly quiz administered and graded by the parent.

Continuous Development

This vocabulary book provides your child a method to learn new vocabulary words. Whenever he encounters an unfamiliar word in his leisure or academic readings, he should examine the word within the context of the reading, and locate it in a dictionary for pronunciation and its appropriate definition. Since this book has six lessons for each nine-week quarter, the student may devote the extra time to his other courses or enjoy leisure reading. Time devoted to leisure reading will continue to expand your child's vocabulary far beyond the words studied in these lessons.

Using the Dictionary and Thesaurus

There are vitally important lessons to be learned in using a dictionary: reviewing alphabetical order past the 1st, 2nd, or 3rd letter; using the Guide Words to locate words; noticing the Guide Words after finding the word; reading and discovering the different meanings one word can have; discovering the different parts of speech for a single word. For the majority of words in this book, words can be found in an intermediate or school dictionary. However, be alert and look for other forms of the word if necessary.

We encourage students to use a thesaurus. A thesaurus contains numerous words with related meanings, each having its own distinct meaning. When your student does any writing, encourage him or her to use a "new" word from the thesaurus. See if you can help your child to understand the small differences in synonyms. An optional thesaurus exercise is suggested in Exercise D. Encourage your student to use or think about different words as you speak together throughout the day. This develops analytical skills.

Finally, we hope you and your student enjoy the playful illustrations in this book.

Introduction

You can learn many new vocabulary words in this text-workbook. You may discover that some of the words are familiar. Some words may be new for you, and other words may be ones that you have misunderstood in the past.

As you go through the lessons, be alert to any words for which you do not recognize their meanings. First, look for these words in a children's dictionary. Perhaps some words have more than one possible meaning. Try to have a grasp of the different meanings of a word. It is not unusual for a word to be both a verb and a noun. For instance, your dictionary will show the word grasp as a noun and as a verb. Your dad might say you have a strong grasp in your handshake, or he may encourage you to grasp the hammer more strongly!

When you read the word in a paragraph, you can easily see if the word is a noun, which is the name of a person, place, or thing. You can easily see if the word is a verb, an action word. Some words can be an adjective as well as a noun. You can play with a football, a noun, but football is an adjective if you are talking about the football coach!

Be alert to the use of words in sentences. See how they are used differently in books and magazines. Listen for your vocabulary words when others speak, and see what the speaker intends to mean. Start using words you don't usually use, and see if you can use them correctly. Be a master of your vocabulary!

This workbook assigns writing a definition for your list words which should demonstrate that you know the meaning of the word. For Exercise B, you need to choose a list word to fit the sentence. Exercises C and D make you think a little more precisely about the meaning of the words. For your further enjoyment, we have included a crossword puzzle for each lesson!

Do not hesitate to be creative and use the vocabulary words in your writing instead of a more common word. Use new words with confidence in your speaking and compositions. If you choose accurate words to say precisely what you mean, your compositions will be more effective. Most of all, have fun with your new words!

Vocabulary Lesson

A Write the dictionary definition for the specific part of speech (noun, verb, adjective, or adverb).

1. handful (n) a small number of people or things

2. vocabulary (n) the range of words that a person uses and understands

3. discover (v) to find something

4. understand (v) To no very well

5. alert (adj) To warn somebody that there might be danger

6. perhaps (adv) maybe or possibly

7. possible (adj) it might happen or be true

8. grasp (v) to seize something and hold it tightly

9. dictionary (n) Lists words in a language in alphad

10. paragraph (n) a short passage in a piece of writing

11. magazine (n) a publication that contains news

12. correctly (adv) True or right

13. demonstrate (v) to show something clealy

14. puzzle (n) something that is hard to understand

15. creative (adj) to use your imagination

B   Write on the line the correct list word to complete each sentence.

Mom said it is ___ that we can attend early Mass on Easter.
My grandma gave me an illustrated ___ to look up the meaning of words.
It is a ___ to me why anyone would miss Mass on Sunday.
I did not ___ the process of long division until my dad helped me.
I ___ the instructions for today's math assignment and can explain them to my sister.
Father Peters told Tom that he said all the Mass responses ___.
Mom said we should not stay up late, or we won't be ___ enough to learn our lessons.
We can enlarge our ___ by reading good books.
My piano teacher wants me to be ___ in trying to play tunes I think of by myself.
I like to roam around the library and try to ___ some new books.

1. possible
2. dictionary
3. puzzle
4. understand
5. grasp
6. correctly
7. alert
8. vocabulary
9. creative
10. discover

C **Circle the correct word.**

1. Which word means a fairly small number?

   a) puzzle   b) vocabulary   c) handful   d) paragraph

2. Which word refers to a thinking process?

   a) vocabulary   b) correctly   c) perhaps   d) creative

3. Which word shows hope?

   a) possible   b) impossible   c) creative   d) alert

4. Which word can cause questions?

   a) understand   b) interrupt   c) paragraph   d) puzzle

5. Which word indicates finding?

   a) demonstrate   b) magazine   c) discover   d) perhaps

D **Circle two words which have either similar or opposite meanings. Write the letter S if they are similar, or O if they are opposite.**

1. vocabulary   list   numbers   words   _S_

2. grasp   defend   understand   handshake   _O_

3. alert   strong   watchful   happy   _OS_

4. creative   pencil   inventive   essay   _S_

5. perhaps   maybe   engage   example   _S_

Optional: Use a thesaurus to find more synonyms and antonyms for the list words.

Use the words from this lesson to complete the crossword puzzle.

ACROSS

4 imaginative
9 publication with stories, articles, and poems
11 show clearly
12 find out
13 able to be done
14 rightly
15 small number

DOWN

1 lay hold of with the mind
2 mystery
3 maybe
5 group of sentences on one topic
6 list of words
7 book giving the meaning of words
8 get the meaning of
10 watchful

Vocabulary Lesson

2

A Write the dictionary definition for the specific part of speech (noun, verb, adjective, or adverb).

1. spring (n) _the season between winter and summer_

2. valley (n) _A dark redish brown color_

3. mountain (n) _a very high piece of land_

4. festival (n) _A celebration or holiday_

5. plush (adj) _very rich and fine_

6. plantation (n) _a large farm_

7. crew (n) _A team of people who work together_

8. maroon (adj) _An area or low ground between tw obil_

9. fabric (n) _1 cloth or material_

10. imagine (v) _To picture something in your mind_

11. form (v) _type or kind_

12. pilot (n) _some one who flies an aircraft_

13. assistant (n) _someone who help's you make things_

14. release (v) _to free someone or something_

15. assemble (v) _to gather together in one place_

B   Write on the line the correct list word to complete each sentence.

Jesus would ___ twelve special men to be His Apostles.	1. Assemble
Betsy Ross used a strong ___ to make the American flag.	2. fabric
The crowd demanded that Pilate ___ Barabbas, not Jesus.	3. release
George Washington called his ___ Mount Vernon.	4. plantation
No one could ___ that Nina had made the wedding dress herself.	5. imagine
The carpet was so ___ that our toddler loved to roll around on it.	6. plush
The Irish ___ on St. Patrick's Day was well attended.	7. festival
Our family likes to hike to the top of that ___ each year.	8. mountain
Charles Lindbergh was the first ___ to fly across the Atlantic Ocean.	9. pilot
Columbus had 40 members of his ___ on the *Santa Maria*.	10. crew

C Circle the correct word.

1. Which word means people coming together for entertainment?

   a) faraway   b.) maroon   c) **festival**   d) cheer

2. Which word is a color?

   a) advertise   b) peculiar   c) reflect   d) **maroon**

3. What word means "collect into one group"?

   a) faraway   b) maroon   c) quiet   d) **assemble**

4. Which of these is a group working together?

   a) **crew**   b) loose   c) crowd   d) form

5. Which word is a time of year?

   a) **spring**   b) fabric   c) valley   d) plantation

D Circle two words which have either similar or opposite meanings. Write the letter S if they are similar, or O if they are opposite.

1. **release**   imagine   fix   **restrain**   ____S____

2. form   crew   **imagine**   **make**   ____S____

3. **crew**   push   plane   **team**   ____S____

4. assistant   **farm**   **release**   plantation   ____O____

5. **assemble**   imagine   viewers   **gather**   ____S____

Optional: Use a thesaurus to find more synonyms and antonyms for the list words.

Use the words from this lesson to complete the crossword puzzle.

ACROSS

2 cloth
9 large area of land where crops are grown
10 mass of land higher than a hill
13 low land between mountains
14 group of people working together
15 soft

DOWN

1 picture in the mind
3 helper
4 person who flies a plane
5 celebration
6 season between winter and summer
7 dark red
8 make
11 gather
12 set free

Vocabulary Lesson

3

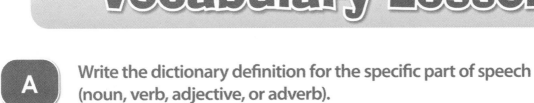

A Write the dictionary definition for the specific part of speech (noun, verb, adjective, or adverb).

1. continent (n) _____

2. avert (v) _____

3. strive (v) _____

4. hero (n) _____

5. desire (v) _____

6. brief (adj) _____

7. future (adj) _____

8. vocation (n) _____

9. companion (n) _____

10. vision (n) _____

11. eager (adj) _____

12. board (v) _____

13. port (n) _____

14. capital (n) _____

15. ordain (v) _____

B Write on the line the correct list word to complete each sentence.

My parents took us on a trip to the nation's __, Washington, DC.	1. _____
The bishop will __ ten new priests tomorrow.	2. _____
The __ of the movie killed the dragon and saved the princess.	3. _____
The soldiers __ to return home.	4. _____
In __ years, most people will be shopping on the Internet.	5. _____
Jesus worked many miracles during the __ time He was on Earth.	6. _____
We should __ to obey the Ten Commandments.	7. _____
The eye doctor determined that Pam's __ was poor.	8. _____
After waiting an hour, we were __ to eat lunch.	9. _____
When he was young, my brother knew his __ was to become a priest.	10. _____

C Circle the correct word.

1. Which word means "to turn away"?

   a) search   b) desired   c) avert   d) strive

2. Which word means "short"?

   a) later   b) brief   c) eager   d) strive

3. Which word means a person of great courage or noble quality?

   a) hero   b) capital   c) vocation   d) companion

4. Which word should you use instead of "try hard"?

   a) capital   b) vocation   c) port   d) strive

5. Which word means a city that is the location of a country's government?

   a) board   b) search   c) void   d) capital

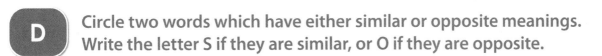 **D** Circle two words which have either similar or opposite meanings. Write the letter S if they are similar, or O if they are opposite.

1. later   avert   avoid   tall   _____

2. career   companion   vocation   vision   _____

3. holy   friendly   companion   enemy   _____

4. future   obey   past   afternoon   _____

5. quit   become   jail   strive   _____

Optional: Use a thesaurus to find more synonyms and antonyms for the list words.

Use the words from this lesson to complete the crossword puzzle.

ACROSS

1 turn away
5 give Holy Orders
6 person of great courage
8 location of a government
9 get on
11 place for ships and boats
13 try hard
14 sight
15 coming after the present

DOWN

2 excited
3 great division of land on the globe
4 calling
7 person who goes with another
10 want
12 short

Vocabulary Lesson

 A Write the dictionary definition for the specific part of speech (noun, verb, adjective, or adverb).

1. chief (adj) _____

2. empire (n) _____

3. trade (n) _____

4. immoral (adj) _____

5. business (n) _____

6. merchant (n) _____

7. distant (adj) _____

8. pagan (adj) _____

9. convert (v) _____

10. crucial (adj) _____

11. slavery (n) _____

12. journey (n) _____

13. rations (n) _____

14. struggle (v) _____

15. assist (v) _____

Write on the line the correct list word to complete each sentence.

Mary and Joseph made a long __ to Egypt with Baby Jesus.	1.
Joseph's brothers sold him as a slave to an Egyptian __.	2.
Jesus helped his foster-father Joseph in his carpentry __.	3.
The __ work of the Apostles resulted in many conversions.	4.
St. Paul went on many journeys to __ places.	5.
Jesus asks us to __ those in need, especially the poorest among us.	6.
The hungry soldiers were grateful for the __ provided by the people.	7.
The little dog began to __ to escape the bear.	8.
In spite of persecution, Christianity spread throughout the Roman __.	9.
In his __ as a mechanic, he repairs cars.	10.

C Circle the correct word.

1. Which word means to change someone's beliefs?

    a) sinful   b) convert   c) chief   d) wrong

2. Which word means "to aid"?

    a) remind   b) assist   c) struggle   d) bring

3. Which word means a person who buys and sells things?

    a) empire   b) rations   c) journey   d) merchant

4. Which word describes a faraway place?

    a) unable   b) sinful   c) distant   d) empire

5. Which word means "long trip"?

    a) journey   b) last   c) short   d) race

D Circle two words which have either similar or opposite meanings. Write the letter S if they are similar, or O if they are opposite.

1. Christian   pagan   avoid   crucial   _____

2. immoral   ease   distant   holy   _____

3. rations   food   right   priest   _____

4. business   temple   trade   assist   _____

5. chief   journey   sadly   unimportant   _____

Optional: Use a thesaurus to find more synonyms and antonyms for the list words.

Use the words from this lesson to complete the crossword puzzle.

ACROSS

5 group of territories under one ruler
6 far away
8 very important
11 person who buys and sells goods
13 help
14 food
15 long trip

DOWN

1 wicked
2 one's work or occupation
3 most important
4 change a person's beliefs
7 the activity of making, buying, and selling
9 bondage
10 make a great effort to do something
12 person who does not know about God

Vocabulary Lesson

A Write the dictionary definition for the specific part of speech (noun, verb, adjective, or adverb).

1. observe (v) _____

2. example (n) _____

3. canoe (n) _____

4. provide (v) _____

5. hold (n) _____

6. terrified (adj) _____

7. mission (n) _____

8. heroic (adj) _____

9. charity (n) _____

10. interpreter (n) _____

11. examine (v) _____

12. tend (v) _____

13. wound (n) _____

14. survive (v) _____

15. welfare (n) _____

Write on the line the correct list word to complete each sentence.

Jesus told Thomas to put his hand into the __ in His side.	1.
After Pentecost, the Apostles were no longer __.	2.
Dad took the boys fishing in his new __.	3.
Mom asked me to be a good __ for my little brothers.	4.
The nurse will __ to my mother while she is in the hospital.	5.
Before confession, we should always __ our conscience.	6.
Judas thought no one would __ him stealing the money.	7.
The sacraments __ us with the grace we need.	8.
The bishop in California accepted the __ to convert the Indians.	9.
The __ soldier gave his life to protect those around him.	10.

C Circle the correct word.

1. Which word means "an injury"?

   a) ill   b) canoe   c) wound   d) tend

2. Which word means "to look at carefully"?

   a) examine   b) provide   c) struggle   d) announce

3. In which of these might you ride?

   a) wound   b) canoe   c) trip   d) example

4. Which word means "to care for"?

   a) terrified   b) tend   c) crowded   d) first

5. Which word could you use instead of "scared"?

   a) first   b) terrified   c) crowded   d) tend

 D Circle two words which have either similar or opposite meanings. Write the letter S if they are similar, or O if they are opposite.

1. observe   overlook   tend   survive   _____

2. provide   warning   kindness   take   _____

3. mission   announce   warning   project   _____

4. heroic   cowardly   examine   charity   _____

5. example   welfare   sample   supply   _____

Optional: Use a thesaurus to find more synonyms and antonyms for the list words.

Use the words from this lesson to complete the crossword puzzle.

ACROSS

2 look at carefully
4 courageous
6 give what is needed
9 long, narrow boat
12 afraid
13 love
15 watch

DOWN

1 remain alive
3 person who translates spoken words
5 injury
7 take care of
8 model to be imitated
10 task or job
11 well-being
14 interior of a ship

Vocabulary Lesson

A Write the dictionary definition for the specific part of speech (noun, verb, adjective, or adverb).

1. vessel (n) _____

2. injure (v) _____

3. instruct (v) _____

4. recite (v) _____

5. judge (v) _____

6. repeat (v) _____

7. cleric (n) _____

8. desert (v) _____

9. owner (n)_____

10. acquire (v) _____

11. daily (adv) _____

12. protect (v) _____

13. frail (adj) _____

14. severely (adv)_____

15. splendid (adj)_____

Write on the line the correct list word to complete each sentence.

He will __ himself playing in that rough football game!	1.
At the end of time, God will __ everyone by his or her behavior.	2.
Any member of the clergy may be called a __.	3.
Though the king would __ great riches, he gave to the poor.	4.
He had been a strong man, but his illness made him __.	5.
"The Last Supper" is a brightly-colored, __ painting in our church.	6.
Many Catholic families pray the Rosary __ after dinner.	7.
St. John did not __ Jesus at the Crucifixion.	8.
The family rented a houseboat and sailed the __ around the coast.	9.
The priest will __ us to prepare for our Confirmation.	10.

Jesus, Mary, Joseph, I love You!

C Circle the correct word.

1. Which word means "to wound"?

   a)   ill   b)   sick   c)   injure   d)   unclean

2. Which word means "extremely"?

   a)   mildly   b)   moderately   c)   severely   d)   calmly

3. Which word relates to a catechism question?

   a)   mistake   b)   recite   c)   desk   d)   honey

4. Which word relates to a purchase?

   a)   owner   b)   steal   c)   judge   d)   library

5. Which word relates to deciding?

   a)   police   b)   burglar   c)   judge   d)   chair

D Circle two words which have either similar or opposite meanings. Write the letter S if they are similar, or O if they are opposite.

1. weasel   ship   vessel   ocean   _____

2. acquire   mirror   charity   lose   _____

3. frail   young   strong   study   _____

4. splendid   dirty   wonderful   examine   _____

5. judge   protect   picture   consider   _____

Optional: Use a thesaurus to find more synonyms and antonyms for the list words.

Use the words from this lesson to complete the crossword puzzle.

ACROSS

3 teach
8 ship
10 leave
12 cause harm
13 keep from being harmed
15 every day

DOWN

1 delicate
2 form an opinion after careful consideration
4 harshly
5 member of the clergy
6 repeat from memory
7 gain
9 impressive in beauty
11 tell again
14 person who owns something

Vocabulary Lesson

7

 A   Write the dictionary definition for the specific part of speech (noun, verb, adjective, or adverb).

1. obvious (adj) _____

2. phony (adj) _____

3. convict (v) _____

4. exile (v) _____

5. clumsy (adj) _____

6. border (n) _____

7. attempt (v) _____

8. risky (adj) _____

9. revive (v) _____

10. vicious (adj) _____

11. decade (n) _____

12. feeble (adj) _____

13. harass (v) _____

14. persecution (n) _____

15. coastline (n) _____

Write on the line the correct list word to complete each sentence.

The strange man tried to trick Dad with his __ story.	1. _____
No one entered their yard because of their __ dog.	2. _____
The soldiers march across the __ to fight the enemy.	3. _____
Catholics in Muslim countries find it __ to be out after dark.	4. _____
The unjust judge would __ Catholics of crimes they did not commit.	5. _____
Unjust governments would __ many Catholic priests and nuns from their country.	6. _____
The math problem was easy, and the answer was __.	7. _____
The __ juggler hit me with the ball!	8. _____
The nasty boys continued to __ the new student.	9. _____
The injured dog made slow, __ movements.	10. _____

C Circle the correct word.

1. Which word means lacking in strength?

    a) unwise   b) clumsy   c) feeble   d) risky

2. Which word means lacking in skill?

    a) unwise   b) clumsy   c) feeble   d) risky

3. What is another word for dangerous?

    a) unwise   b) clumsy   c) feeble   d) risky

4. What is a word for forcing a person from his own country?

    a) police   b) exile   c) phony   d) border

5. Which word should you use instead of "easily understood"?

    a) convict   b) vicious   c) wicked   d) obvious

D Circle two words which have either similar or opposite meanings. Write the letter S if they are similar, or O if they are opposite.

1. feeble   exile   border   strong   _____

2. kind   convict   vicious   bright   _____

3. obvious   attempt   unclear   vicious   _____

4. try   feeble   warning   attempt   _____

5. border   jail   boundary   elegant   _____

Optional: Use a thesaurus to find more synonyms and antonyms for the list words.

ACROSS

5 try to do
6 prove guilty
7 annoy again and again
9 dangerous
10 lacking strength
11 continual cruel treatment
14 easily understood
15 boundary

DOWN

1 boundary between land and ocean
2 period of ten years
3 not real or genuine
4 force someone to leave his own country
8 violent and cruel
12 bring back into use
13 lacking skill in movement

Vocabulary Lesson

 A   Write the dictionary definition for the specific part of speech (noun, verb, adjective, or adverb).

1. construction (n) _____

2. seize (v) _____

3. trample (v) _____

4. government (n) _____

5. resume (v) _____

6. operate (v) _____

7. process (n) _____

8. structure (n) _____

9. restore (v) _____

10. present (adj) _____

11. extend (v) _____

12. conquer (v) _____

13. occupy (v) _____

14. warehouse (n) _____

15. century (n) _____

B   Write on the line the correct list word to complete each sentence.

The soldiers planned to __ Our Lord in the Garden of Gethsemane.	1. _____
The __ of the new hospital was delayed because of bad weather.	2. _____
After lunch, we will __ our vocabulary lessons.	3. _____
My dad explained the __ for making steel in the factory.	4. _____
Our family will __ the rental house for the summer.	5. _____
Our home was damaged by the flood; the workers will __ it to look like new.	6. _____
The hardware store keeps the extra supplies in the __.	7. _____
Dad showed my older brother how to __ the electric mower.	8. _____
In the last __, doctors have discovered cures for many diseases.	9. _____
No one believed that William, the Norman leader, could __ the English at the Battle of Hastings.	10. _____

C Circle the correct word.

1. Which word means "to take by force"?

   a) open   b) seize   c) trample   d) operate

2. Which word refers to using a machine?

   a) open   b) seize   c) trample   d) operate

3. What is another word for "crush"?

   a) open   b) seize   c) trample   d) operate

4. What is another word for "continue"?

   a) restore   b) permit   c) resume   d) building

5. Which word may you use instead of "the process of building"?

   a) restore   b) permit   c) resume   d) construction

D Circle two words which have either similar or opposite meanings. Write the letter S if they are similar, or O if they are opposite.

1. present   cheery   cheek   absent   _____

2. building   process   structure   yard   _____

3. watch   seize   extend   shorten   _____

4. defeat   seize   soldier   conquer   _____

5. process   conquer   resume   procedure   _____

Optional: Use a thesaurus to find more synonyms and antonyms for the list words.

ACROSS

1 return to good condition
5 overcome
7 one hundred years
10 series of actions leading to a result
12 stretch out
13 crush under the feet
14 something built in a definite way

DOWN

2 live in as a tenant
3 building for storing goods
4 begin again
5 the process of building
6 political rule
8 being here and not elsewhere
9 work in a proper way
11 take by force

Vocabulary Lesson

A Write the dictionary definition for the specific part of speech (noun, verb, adjective, or adverb).

1. inquire (v) _____

2. inform (v) _____

3. admire (v) _____

4. associate (n) _____

5. reside (v) _____

6. monastery (n) _____

7. toil (v) _____

8. abbot (n) _____

9. consider (v) _____

10. request (v) _____

11. discipline (n) _____

12. regret (v) _____

13. scoundrel (n) _____

14. plot (v) _____

15. repent (v) _____

B   Write on the line the correct list word to complete each sentence.

Americans __ Washington for his determination to win freedom.	1. _____
American presidents __ in the White House.	2. _____
General Lafayette was a very close __ of George Washington.	3. _____
Farmers __ each day to produce good crops.	4. _____
The American colonies were forced to __ help from France.	5. _____
Was Benedict Arnold a hero or a __?	6. _____
For true contrition, we tell God that we __ having sinned.	7. _____
The soldiers hated to __ Washington of Arnold's treason.	8. _____
The __ was in charge of the abbey for many years.	9. _____
With an important decision, __ your choices carefully.	10. _____

C Circle the correct word.

1. Which word means "to tell about"?

   a) inquire   b) inform   c) regret   d) consider

2. Which word means "to feel sorry or unhappy"?

   a) inquire   b) inform   c) regret   d) consider

3. What is another word for "ask"?

   a) inquire   b) inform   c) regret   d) consider

4. What is another word for "plan secretly"?

   a) consider   b) plot   c) toil   d) request

5. Which word may you use instead of "work"?

   a) regret   b) rescue   c) toil   d) admire

D Circle two words which have either similar or opposite meanings. Write the letter S if they are similar, or O if they are opposite.

1. associate   abbot   friend   child   _____

2. instant   villain   scoundrel   pudding   _____

3. consider   admire   inform   tell   _____

4. plot   plan   warn   abandon   _____

5. admire   dislike   require   test   _____

Optional: Use a thesaurus to find more synonyms and antonyms for the list words.

Use the words from this lesson to complete the crossword puzzle.

ACROSS

1 be sorry for having sinned
3 person with whom one works
6 ask about
9 wicked person
11 ask for something
13 think very highly of
14 place where monks live

DOWN

1 be sorry
2 work hard
4 think over carefully
5 let a person know something
7 training that corrects or strengthens
8 head of an abbey
10 dwell
12 plan

Vocabulary Lesson

A Write the dictionary definition for the specific part of speech (noun, verb, adjective, or adverb).

1. annual (adj) _____

2. confection (n) _____

3. ceramic (adj) _____

4. platter (n) _____

5. gasp (v) _____

6. angle (n) _____

7. wondrous (adj) _____

8. chef (n) _____

9. batter (n) _____

10. peppermint (n) _____

11. puff (n) _____

12. revolve (v) _____

13. chance (n) _____

14. digestion (n) _____

15. complaint (n) _____

B   Write on the line the correct list word to complete each sentence.

The __ has a special recipe for his apple pie.	1.
Which __ do you like best: cakes, pies, or candy?	2.
Juan Diego would __ in awe at the sight of the Blessed Mother.	3.
Our family makes an __ pilgrimage to the Marian shrine.	4.
Dad said he would not listen to a single __ about our trip.	5.
Is there any more __ miracle than the Miracle of the Sun at Fatima?	6.
Do all merry-go-rounds __ in the same direction?	7.
Add blueberries to the pancake __ in the blue bowl.	8.
Mom likes to grow __ to make a strong flavored ice tea.	9.
I took lessons so I could make __ plates and bowls.	10.

C Circle the correct word.

1. Which word is the opposite of "praise"?

    a)   annual   b)   evening   c)   batter   d)   complaint

2. Which word indicates how often one has a birthday party?

    a)   annual   b)   evening   c)   batter   d)   complaint

3. What word would you most associate with a cookbook?

    a)   batter   b)   revolve   c)   inspect   d)   unusual

4. Which of these can you eat?

    a)   restaurant   b)   evening   c)   complaint   d)   confection

5. Which word is something a surprised person does?

    a)   revolved   b)   waiting   c)   inspect   d)   gasp

D Circle two words which have either similar or opposite meanings. Write the letter S if they are similar, or O if they are opposite.

1. platter   batter   revolve   dish   _____

2. annual   gasp   yearly   grasp   _____

3. late   amazing   wait   wondrous   _____

4. scout   recipe   dessert   confection   _____

5. rotate   remote   revolve   restaurant   _____

Optional: Use a thesaurus to find more synonyms and antonyms for the list words.

Use the words from this lesson to complete the crossword puzzle.

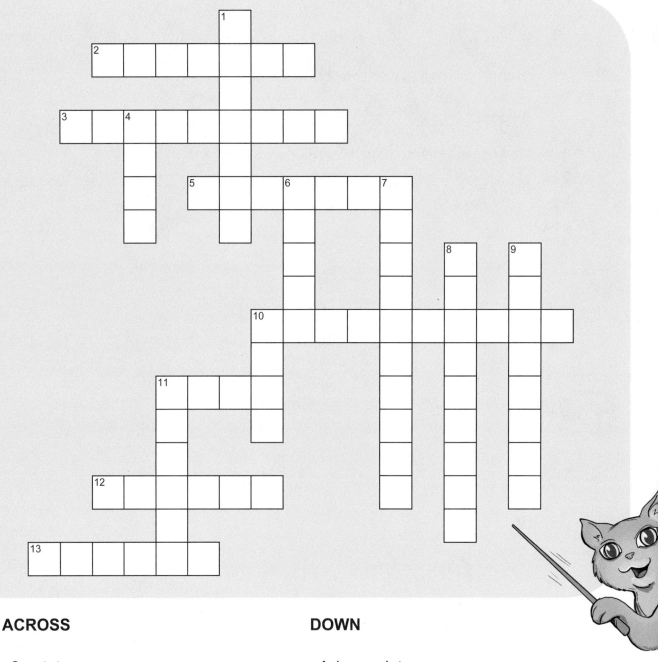

ACROSS

2 rotate
3 the body's process of changing food
5 made of baked clay
10 plant used in flavoring
11 cook
12 happening once a year
13 mixture of flour and liquid for cooking

DOWN

1 large plate
4 breathe in suddenly
6 two lines meeting at a point
7 fancy, sweet food
8 expression of discontent
9 marvelous
10 light pastry
11 opportunity

Vocabulary Lesson

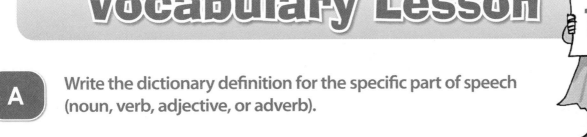

A   Write the dictionary definition for the specific part of speech (noun, verb, adjective, or adverb).

1. cruise (n) _____

2. ancient (adj) _____

3. dependable (adj) _____

4. inventor (n) _____

5. fascinating (adj) _____

6. schooner (n) _____

7. entertainment (n) _____

8. destination (n)_____

9. sight (n) _____

10. modernize (v) _____

11. steady (adj) _____

12. reasonable (adj) _____

13. occupant (n) _____

14. brilliant (adj) _____

15. voyage (n) _____

Write on the line the correct list word to complete each sentence.

The furniture factory intends to __ its old machines.	1.
The __ lights lit up the beautiful life-size Nativity scene.	2.
When my cousin rode across the country on his bicycle, it took him two months to reach his __.	3.
It was __ to see the watchmaker as he carefully fixed my watch.	4.
We saw many beautiful sights on our relaxing ocean __.	5.
In Rome, Nina wanted to see the __ ruins.	6.
No __ was allowed to smoke in the hotel room.	7.
The __ flow of water from the stream provided daily fresh water.	8.
Andy is a __ altar boy; he is never late to Mass.	9.
St. Paul went on many a dangerous __ at sea!	10.

Jesus, Mary, Joseph, I love You!

C Circle the correct word.

1. Which word is the opposite of "modern"?

   a) ancient   b) exciting   c) steady   d) rough

2. Which word means a kind of ship?

   a) ancient   b) exciting   c) steady   d) schooner

3. What word means "regular"?

   a) ancient   b) exciting   c) steady   d) rough

4. Which of these may have a seat in an airplane?

   a) voyage   b) weather   c) narrow   d) occupant

5. Which word should you use to describe a magic trick?

   a) ancient   b) narrow   c) steady   d) fascinating

D Circle two words which have either similar or opposite meanings. Write the letter S if they are similar, or O if they are opposite.

1. reasonable   wide   logical   colorful   _____

2. dependable   travel   weather   reliable   _____

3. boring   destination   goal   please   _____

4. entertainment   schooner   amusement   occupant   _____

5. ancient   library   old   sights   _____

Optional: Use a thesaurus to find more synonyms and antonyms for the list words.

ACROSS

2 make suitable for the present time
5 something seen
6 pleasure trip on a ship
8 extremely interesting
12 amusement
13 one who is inside
14 very bright
15 reliable

DOWN

1 ship with two masts
3 sensible
4 long journey by water
7 showing little change
9 person who thinks up new things
10 very old
11 goal of a journey

Vocabulary Lesson

A Write the dictionary definition for the specific part of speech (noun, verb, adjective, or adverb).

1. guide (n) _____

2. tour (v) _____

3. determine (v) _____

4. sculptor (n) _____

5. stubborn (adj) _____

6. accommodate (v) _____

7. objective (n) _____

8. barrier (n) _____

9. panel (n) _____

10. illustrate (v) _____

11. scene (n) _____

12. prophet (n) _____

13. predict (v) _____

14. Messiah (n) _____

15. talent (n) _____

Write on the line the correct list word to complete each sentence.

The jury will __ whether he is innocent or guilty.	1.
Since Pharaoh remained __, God sent the Ten Plagues.	2.
The pillar of cloud acted as a __ between the Israelites and the Egyptian army.	3.
The __ carved an angel from white marble.	4.
Dad began to explain and __ the process of long division.	5.
Peter's __ was to protect Jesus from the Roman soldiers.	6.
The __ Daniel predicted the death of the king of Babylon.	7.
The __ at the shrine showed them the Stations of the Cross.	8.
We arranged to __ the catacombs, where we prayed.	9.
The convent in Rome will __ the Catholic students.	10.

C Circle the correct word.

1. Which word means "to make clear"?

   a) expect   b) cover   c) illustrate   d) predict

2. Which word means "one to save His people"?

   a) clear   b) aim   c) goal   d) Messiah

3. What word means "to tell the future"?

   a) predict   b) aided   c) only   d) alone

4. What do we call one who makes statues?

   a) cover   b) plain   c) intention   d) sculptor

5. Which word means "to provide with a place to stay"?

   a) show   b) hide   c) predict   d) accommodate

D Circle two words which have either similar or opposite meanings. Write the letter S if they are similar, or O if they are opposite.

1. barrier   demand   defend   fence   _____

2. leader   map   mask   guide   _____

3. aim   final   scene   objective   _____

4. prophet   panel   skill   talent   _____

5. stubborn   boring   agreeable   limited   _____

Optional: Use a thesaurus to find more synonyms and antonyms for the list words.

Use the words from this lesson to complete the crossword puzzle.

ACROSS

2 rectangular section
3 travel from place to place
4 deliverer of God's Chosen People
9 person who declares a message from God
10 clarify
12 someone that shows the way
13 refusing to change
14 view that resembles a picture

DOWN

1 come to a decision
2 foretell
5 provide with a place to stay
6 goal
7 something that blocks the way
8 special ability
11 person who makes statues

Vocabulary Lesson

A Write the dictionary definition for the specific part of speech (noun, verb, adjective, or adverb).

1. patron (n) _____

2. royal (adj) _____

3. passion (n) _____

4. hunt (n) _____

5. chapel (n) _____

6. expedition (n) _____

7. pursue (v) _____

8. issue (v) _____

9. transform (v) _____

10. moral (adj) _____

11. diocese (n) _____

12. advise (v) _____

13. kingdom (n) _____

14. property (n) _____

15. donate (v) _____

B Write on the line the correct list word to complete each sentence.

Who is the bishop of your __ ?	1.
Did you __ to the missions for the poor?	2.
We went to Mass at a small __ dedicated to the Sacred Heart.	3.
Queen Isabel of Spain ruled her __ for thirty years.	4.
The Ten Commandments are our guide to live a __ life.	5.
God is happy with former sinners who worked to __ their lives.	6.
The shepherd went to __ the missing sheep.	7.
The king and queen rode in the __ carriage in the parade.	8.
For Confirmation, I chose St. Joseph as my __.	9.
Every year, Dad takes us on a __ for moose in Canada.	10.

Jesus, Mary, Joseph, I love You!

C | Circle the correct word.

1. Which word means "good"?

    a) royal   b) crucifix   c) moral   d) sparkling

2. Which word means "to change"?

    a) donate   b) property   c) live   d) transform

3. Which word relates to "royal"?

    a) kingdom   b) hunting   c) advise   d) chapel

4. What is another word for "land"?

    a) chapel   b) donate   c) royal   d) property

5. Which word relates to a bishop?

    a) donate   b) sparkling   c) passion   d) diocese

D | Circle two words which have either similar or opposite meanings. Write the letter S if they are similar, or O if they are opposite.

1. passion   donate   zeal   transform   _____

2. donate   kingdom   keep   church   _____

3. journey   desire   expedition   gift   _____

4. thinking   pursue   follow   train   _____

5. advise   ignore   donate   moral   _____

Optional: Use a thesaurus to find more synonyms and antonyms for the list words.

Use the words from this lesson to complete the crossword puzzle.

ACROSS

3 a search
4 something that is owned
8 relating to a king or queen
9 flow out
13 give suggestions
14 journey
15 virtuous

DOWN

1 give away
2 special guardian
5 change completely
6 area under the authority of a bishop
7 chase
10 country ruled by a king or queen
11 strong emotion
12 small church

Vocabulary Lesson

A   Write the dictionary definition for the specific part of speech (noun, verb, adjective, or adverb).

1. adjustable (adj) _____

2. skilled (adj) _____

3. wealthy (adj) _____

4. purchase (v) _____

5. detail (n) _____

6. religious (adj) _____

7. cathedral (n) _____

8. nave (n) _____

9. tabernacle (n) _____

10. vivid (adj) _____

11. gratitude (n) _____

12. erect (v) _____

13. overlook (v) _____

14. depart (v) _____

15. courtyard (n)_____

B   Write on the line the correct list word to complete each sentence.

We can find beautiful __ paintings in Catholic churches.	1.
Our bishop's __ has many stained glass windows.	2.
The bookshelves are __ so that they can hold books of different sizes.	3.
The priest placed the Eucharist into the golden __.	4.
The Jesuit Order would __ many of Rubens' religious paintings.	5.
It is rare to find dedicated and __ religious artists today.	6.
Many __ Catholics have supported the expensive art in churches.	7.
Most people like the __ colors of stained glass windows.	8.
That church has Stations of the Cross in the outside __.	9.
Do not __ all the colorful details in that stained glass window.	10.

C Circle the correct word.

1. Which word means "bright"?

   a)   wealthy   b)   vivid   c)   skilled   d)   wealthy

2. Which word means "to leave"?

   a)   overlook   b)   purchase   c)   depart   d)   nave

3. In which of these is the Holy Eucharist kept?

   a)   depart   b)   painting   c)   nave   d)   tabernacle

4. Which word means "to buy"?

   a)   depart   b)   overlook   c)   purchase   d)   painting

5. Which word might you use instead of "rich"?

   a)   money   b)   painter   c)   skilled   d)   wealthy

D Circle two words which have either similar or opposite meanings.
Write the letter S if they are similar, or O if they are opposite.

1. gratitude   Bible   marble   appreciation   _____

2. erect   skilled   talented   cook   _____

3. religious   court   pious   garden   _____

4. painting   observe   brush   overlook   _____

5. senators   church   military   cathedral   _____

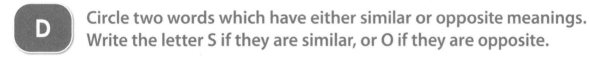

Optional: Use a thesaurus to find more synonyms and antonyms for the list words.

Use the words from this lesson to complete the crossword puzzle.

ACROSS

1 put up
3 small part of something larger
8 fail to see
10 feeling of appreciation
12 contains the Blessed Sacrament
14 having ability
15 leave

DOWN

2 main church of a diocese
4 able to be changed
5 devoted to God
6 enclosed space next to a building
7 central part of a church
9 buy
11 rich
13 very bright

Vocabulary Lesson

15

 **A** Write the dictionary definition for the specific part of speech (noun, verb, adjective, or adverb).

1. wander (v) _____

2. parrot (n) _____

3. branch (n) _____

4. pastry (n) _____

5. yearn (v) _____

6. deter (v) _____

7. scheme (v) _____

8. pretend (v) _____

9. precious (adj) _____

10. satisfy (v) _____

11. scurry (v) _____

12. foolish (adj) _____

13. fowl (n) _____

14. furious (adj) _____

15. weep (v) _____

B   Write on the line the correct list word to complete each sentence.

The __ high priest tore his clothes when Jesus said He was the Son of God.	1.
God made the Hebrews __ in the desert for forty years.	2.
My grandma made a delicious __ for Christmas.	3.
Satan did __ to trick Adam and Eve into disobedience.	4.
Satan decided to __ that he was Eve's friend.	5.
Eve suddenly reached up to the __ and took the forbidden fruit.	6.
Adam and Eve lost the __ gifts that God had given them.	7.
Uncle Jack loved to hunt geese, duck, and other delicious __.	8.
Joan of Arc let nothing __ her from seeing the French king.	9.
When Jesus saw the crying women, He said, "Do not __ for Me."	10.

C Circle the correct word.

1. Which word shows what a sad person would do?

    a) wander   b) scurry   c) pretend   d) weep

2. Which word means "to desire"?

    a) wander   b) yearn   c) pretend   d) weep

3. Which word is the opposite of "worthless"?

    a) foolish   b) furious   c) satisfy   d) precious

4. Which of these words means "to stop"?

    a) scheme   b) pretend   c) deter   d) scurry

5. Which word would you use when writing about someone silly?

    a) parrot   b) foolish   c) fowl   d) furious

 D Circle two words which have either similar or opposite meanings. Write the letter S if they are similar, or O if they are opposite.

1. scurry   rush   brush   hush   _____

2. plan   stream   scheme   steam   _____

3. lamb   branch   limb   ranch   _____

4. wander   walk   talk   chalk   _____

5. claim   calm   clam   furious   _____

Optional: Use a thesaurus to find more synonyms and antonyms for the list words.

Use the words from this lesson to complete the crossword puzzle.

ACROSS

2 walk without a purpose
4 grows out from the trunk of a tree
5 cry
8 a bird
9 valuable
11 form a secret plan
12 brightly colored bird
13 desire something very much
14 make someone content

DOWN

1 very angry
3 prevent from acting
6 sweet baked good
7 move quickly
9 make believe
10 lacking good sense

Vocabulary Lesson

A Write the dictionary definition for the specific part of speech (noun, verb, adjective, or adverb).

1. autumn (n) _____

2. warmth (n) _____

3. distance (n) _____

4. nearer (adv) _____

5. impassable (adj) _____

6. valuable (adj) _____

7. startle (v) _____

8. section (n) _____

9. crouch (v) _____

10. scramble (v) _____

11. trellis (n) _____

12. banquet (n) _____

13. farther (adv) _____

14. capable (adj) _____

15. gloomy (adj) _____

B   Write on the line the correct list word to complete each sentence.

In late __, we celebrate All Saints' Day and Thanksgiving.	1.
As the Magi traveled __ to Bethlehem, the star became brighter.	2.
Because of the snow storm, the mountain road became __.	3.
The little boy intended to __ his sisters with his Halloween mask!	4.
As the arrows began to fly, the cowboys ran to __ behind a boulder.	5.
Jesus worked His first miracle during a wedding __ at Cana.	6.
My dad grew the best red grapes over a large __ in our backyard.	7.
The children __ for the falling candy.	8.
Aunt Betty brought me a rare, __ relic of St. Therese.	9.
Going __ along the shore, Jesus saw John mending his fishing nets.	10.

Jesus, Mary, Joseph, I love You!

C Circle the correct word.

1. Where would you find food?

   a) autumn   b) warmth   c) gloomy   d) banquet

2. Which word relates to something that is far away?

   a) trellis   b) section   c) distance   d) gloomy

3. What word is the opposite of "coolness"?

   a) startled   b) trellis   c) gloomy   d) warmth

4. Which word means "closer"?

   a) autumn   b) section   c) trellis   d) nearer

5. Which word might you use when writing about someone sad?

   a) capable   b) gloomy   c) startled   d) valuable

D Circle two words which have either similar or opposite meanings. Write the letter S if they are similar, or O if they are opposite.

1. farther   capable   nearer   valuable   _____

2. startle   surprise   dense   sense   _____

3. eggs   autumn   spring   scrambled   _____

4. valuable   gems   rocky   cheap   _____

5. section   peas   piece   peace   _____

Optional: Use a thesaurus to find more synonyms and antonyms for the list words.

Use the words from this lesson to complete the crossword puzzle.

ACROSS

2 gentle heat
4 frighten suddenly but slightly
6 impossible to cross
8 sad
9 how far apart two things are
11 division of a thing
13 of great worth
14 at a greater distance
15 lattice frame

DOWN

1 able to accomplish something
3 season between summer and winter
5 stoop or bend low
7 formal dinner
10 move or climb quickly
12 closer

Vocabulary Lesson

A Write the dictionary definition for the specific part of speech (noun, verb, adjective, or adverb).

1. humorous (adj) _____

2. amusing (adj) _____

3. annoying (adj) _____

4. occasion (n) _____

5. eyesight (n) _____

6. arrange (v) _____

7. encouraging (adj) _____

8. fleet (adj) _____

9. specimen (n) _____

10. intention (n) _____

11. slower (adv) _____

12. creep (v) _____

13. hopeful (adj) _____

14. faint (adj) _____

15. respond (v) _____

Write on the line the correct list word to complete each sentence.

One of Jesus' miracles was to restore ___ to the blind man.	1.
We ___ our books in alphabetical order.	2.
The little baby found it ___ to play peek-a-boo.	3.
Mark Twain is known for his ___ story about the jumping frog race.	4.
The children were ___ that it would snow on Christmas.	5.
The monarch is a well-known ___ of butterfly.	6.
On what ___ did the Apostles baptize 3,000 people?	7.
Peter ran ___ than young John, who arrived at the tomb first.	8.
Today, we watched our cat, Whiskers, ___ silently up to a mouse.	9.
That dog has an ___ habit of barking early in the morning.	10.

C Circle the correct word.

1. Which word means quick or swift?

   a) molasses b) fleet c) creep d) faint

2. Which word means an example?

   a) creep b) specimen c) faint d) occasion

3. What word means irritating?

   a) hopeful b) arrange c) annoying d) respond

4. Which word means entertaining?

   a) amusing b) faint c) hopeful d) encouraging

5. Which word means an event?

   a) creep b) slower c) occasion d) hopeful

D Circle two words which have either similar or opposite meanings. Write the letter S if they are similar, or O if they are opposite.

1. specimen funny intention humorous _____

2. slower last rarer faster _____

3. event tine occasion tin _____

4. intention gleam game goal _____

5. reply refuse recall respond _____

Optional: Use a thesaurus to find more synonyms and antonyms for the list words.

Use the words from this lesson to complete the crossword puzzle.

ACROSS

3 special event
6 aim
7 answer
9 to move slowly or quietly
10 having hope
12 entertaining
14 example
15 funny

DOWN

1 giving confidence
2 not clear
4 vision
5 irritating
8 put in order
11 swift
13 moving with less speed

Vocabulary Lesson

A Write the dictionary definition for the specific part of speech (noun, verb, adjective, or adverb).

1. fictional (adj) _____

2. advice (n) _____

3. educational (adj) _____

4. classic (adj) _____

5. conduct (n) _____

6. disguise (v) _____

7. garment (n) _____

8. wardrobe (n) _____

9. offer (v) _____

10. support (v) _____

11. embrace (v) _____

12. orderly (adj) _____

13. remove (v) _____

14. pulpit (n) _____

15. professor (n) _____

Write on the line the correct list word to complete each sentence.

The __ and his students at the Catholic college attend daily Mass.	1. _____
Father Pro would __ his appearance during the Mexican attacks on priests.	2. _____
I like to read true stories more than __ stories.	3. _____
Mary went to visit and to __ her cousin Elizabeth.	4. _____
Reading the encyclopedia is of great __ benefit.	5. _____
Mother told us to arrange our school supplies in an __ way.	6. _____
In the confessional, we can ask the priest for __ to be good.	7. _____
Dad praised us for our good __ at Mass.	8. _____
Jesus expects us to __ bad habits and practice good habits.	9. _____
We __ our parish church with a weekly donation.	10. _____

Jesus, Mary, Joseph, I love You!

C Circle the correct word.

1. Which do you do when you see your parents?

   a) disguise   b) remove   c) embrace   d) classic

2. Which word means "to hide"?

   a) advice   b) offer   c) disguise   d) remove

3. What word means "to get rid of"?

   a) remove   b) classic   c) offer   d) pulpit

4. Which of these words means "neat"?

   a) advice   b) wardrobe   c) garment   d) orderly

5. Which word is the opposite of "real"?

   a) classic   b) fictional   c) advice   d) educational

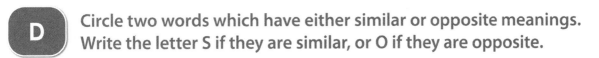 **D** Circle two words which have either similar or opposite meanings. Write the letter S if they are similar, or O if they are opposite.

1. clothes   conduct   classic   wardrobe   _____

2. orderly   new   tidy   next   _____

3. professor   priest   rancher   teacher   _____

4. offer   support   soup   present   _____

5. advice   new   conduct   behavior   _____

Optional: Use a thesaurus to find more synonyms and antonyms for the list words.

Use the words from this lesson to complete the crossword puzzle.

ACROSS

2 assist
7 personal behavior
10 judged to be of timeless quality, among the best of its kind
11 the clothes a person owns
12 tidy
13 get rid of
14 suggestions
15 having to do with learning

DOWN

1 hide
3 teacher
4 to present
5 hug
6 raised platform for preaching
8 made-up
9 article of clothing

Vocabulary Lesson

19

A Write the dictionary definition for the specific part of speech (noun, verb, adjective, or adverb).

1. congregation (n) _____

2. solemn (adj) _____

3. melody (n) _____

4. column (n) _____

5. colorful (adj) _____

6. banish (v) _____

7. equipment (n) _____

8. embroider (v) _____

9. liberate (v) _____

10. navigate (v) _____

11. shore (n) _____

12. encircle (v) _____

13. miter (n) _____

14. crozier (n) _____

15. parish (n) _____

Write on the line the correct list word to complete each sentence.

As the Apostles __ their boat across the lake, Jesus sleeps.	1.
The bishop's __ shows he is like a shepherd of his people.	2.
St. Augustine in St. Augustine, Florida is the oldest __ in the United States.	3.
When the bishop entered the church, the entire __ rose.	4.
When adding double digits, add the ones __ first.	5.
Soldiers use special __, such as shields and helmets, to protect themselves.	6.
Before he sat down, Bishop Roberts carefully took off his __.	7.
The angel was sent to __ St. Peter from prison.	8.
Nina will __ her wedding dress with a hundred pearls.	9.
Stephen was crowned king of Hungary in a __ ceremony.	10.

Jesus, Mary, Joseph, I love You!

C Circle the correct word.

1. Which word would relate to soldiers attacking an enemy camp?

   a) colorful   b) miter   c) encircle   d) shores

2. Which word means "to free"?

   a) encircle   b) banish   c) liberate   d) parish

3. What word is the opposite of "dull"?

   a) dusty   b) rusty   c) crozier   d) colorful

4. Which of these words means "to exile"?

   a) banish   b) encircle   c) navigate   d) embroider

5. Where would you find a beach?

   a) melody   b) column   c) shore   d) congregation

D Circle two words which have either similar or opposite meanings. Write the letter S if they are similar, or O if they are opposite.

1. column   parish   shore   row   _____

2. song   miter   melody   train   _____

3. tools   twos   toes   equipment   _____

4. encircle   romp   ring   crozier   _____

5. stir   stare   navigate   steer   _____

Optional: Use a thesaurus to find more synonyms and antonyms for the list words.

CROSSWORD PUZZLE Use the words from this lesson to complete the crossword puzzle.

ACROSS

2 set free
4 land along the edge of water
5 decorate with needlework
7 bishop's staff
8 having bright colors
11 steer a course
12 bishop's cap
13 serious and dignified
14 force to leave

DOWN

1 pleasing arrangement of sounds
3 assembly of persons
5 tools
6 surround
9 part of a diocese under authority of a priest
10 long row

Vocabulary Lesson

Write the dictionary definition for the specific part of speech (noun, verb, adjective, or adverb).

1. theater (n) _____

2. advertise (v) _____

3. confuse (v) _____

4. eerie (adj) _____

5. peculiar (adj) _____

6. tempest (n) _____

7. jagged (adj) _____

8. reflect (v) _____

9. dance (n) _____

10. rehearse (v) _____

11. perilous (adj) _____

12. platform (n) _____

13. fantastic (adj) _____

14. straight (adv) _____

15. disagree (v) _____

Write on the line the correct list word to complete each sentence.

Mother told us to come __ home after the Cinderella movie.	1.
Did Cinderella's sudden departure __ the prince?	2.
The prince began to __ all over the kingdom to find Cinderella.	3.
Cinderella felt __ when the prince found her.	4.
The hunter heard the __ noises of strange beasts in the forest.	5.
After Our Lord died on Calvary, __ cracks appeared in the Earth.	6.
As the Apostles sailed their boat across the lake, a wild __ struck!	7.
In that __ storm, Jesus told His Apostles not to fear.	8.
The homeschooled students must __ their play for many weeks.	9.
His poor dance performance did not __ his true ability.	10.

C Circle the correct word.

1. Which word means "a storm"?

   a) theater　　　b) tempest　　　c) dancer　　　d) platform

2. Which word would you most likely use to talk about a mirror?

   a) advertise　　　b) peculiar　　　c) reflect　　　d) eerie

3. What word is the opposite of "smooth"?

   a) eerie　　　b) peculiar　　　c) jagged　　　d) fantastic

4. Which of these words means "to announce"?

   a) disagree　　　b) confuse　　　c) rehearse　　　d) advertise

5. Which word would you use when writing about something dangerous?

   a) perilous　　　b) straight　　　c) theater　　　d) peculiar

D Circle two words which have either similar or opposite meanings. Write the letter S if they are similar, or O if they are opposite.

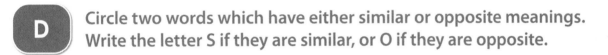

1. peculiar　　　odd　　　jagged　　　jug　　　_____

2. crooked　　　narrow　　　stage　　　platform　　　_____

3. dance　　　confuse　　　clarify　　　danger　　　_____

4. practice　　　remember　　　rewind　　　rehearse　　　_____

5. eerie　　　strange　　　strained　　　trained　　　_____

Optional: Use a thesaurus to find more synonyms and antonyms for the list words.

Use the words from this lesson to complete the crossword puzzle.

ACROSS

1 sharply uneven
3 raised floor
8 strong wind
9 series of movements in time to music
11 odd
12 differ in opinion
13 where plays are presented
14 dangerous
15 extremely good

DOWN

2 causing uneasiness
4 give back an image
5 in a direct manner, course, or line
6 announce publicly
7 make uncertain
10 practice

Jesus, Mary, Joseph, I love You!

Vocabulary Lesson

 A Write the dictionary definition for the specific part of speech (noun, verb, adjective, or adverb).

1. healthy (adj) _____

2. roam (v) _____

3. lonely (adj) _____

4. escape (v) _____

5. vow (v) _____

6. carcass (n) _____

7. buzzard (n) _____

8. stumble (v) _____

9. damage (v) _____

10. separate (v) _____

11. deplete (v) _____

12. approach (v) _____

13. delighted (adj) _____

14. gnaw (v) _____

15. debt (n) _____

Write on the line the correct list word to complete each sentence.

Did the nun __ to be obedient when she entered the convent?	1.
Little Red Riding Hood was barely able to __ the Big Bad Wolf.	2.
Jesus began to __ under the weight of the Cross.	3.
As Jesus carried His Cross, some women tried to __ Him.	4.
The heavy Cross caused Jesus' strength to __.	5.
The brave knight would __ his sword while fighting for France.	6.
Hansel and Gretel knew that wild beasts would __ the forest.	7.
The poor man did not have the money to pay his __.	8.
In the sky, we saw a __ circling over a dead animal in the field.	9.
Mother said that to stay __, I should eat all my vegetables.	10.

C **Circle the correct word.**

1. Which word means "happy"?

   a)   roam   b)   vow   c)   delighted   d)   depleted

2. Which word means "to promise"?

   a)   vow   b)   gnaw   c)   debt   d)   escape

3. What word means "to chew"?

   a)   gnaw   b)   escape   c)   roam   d)   deplete

4. Which of these words means "to flee"?

   a)   approach   b)   deplete   c)   escape   d)   roam

5. Which word describes someone well?

   a)   debt   b)   healthy   c)   buzzard   d)   lonely

 D **Circle two words which have either similar or opposite meanings. Write the letter S if they are similar, or O if they are opposite.**

1. damage   repair   do   dew   _____

2. roam   ream   settle   rein   _____

3. approach   lonely   remove   alone   _____

4. buzzer   roam   buzzard   vulture   _____

5. join   attack   joy   separate   _____

Optional: Use a thesaurus to find more synonyms and antonyms for the list words.

Use the words from this lesson to complete the crossword puzzle.

ACROSS

2 set apart
3 pleased
7 large bird of prey
10 cause harm
12 come near
13 wander
14 not often visited
15 trip

DOWN

1 get away
4 something owed
5 sound and well
6 bite or chew upon
8 dead body of an animal
9 reduce in amount by using up
11 make a solemn promise

Vocabulary Lesson

A Write the dictionary definition for the specific part of speech (noun, verb, adjective, or adverb).

1. custodian (n) _____

2. eccentric (adj) _____

3. blouse (n) _____

4. discuss (v) _____

5. container (n) _____

6. carving (n) _____

7. incentive (n) _____

8. salary (n) _____

9. novice (n) _____

10. prosper (v) _____

11. policy (n) _____

12. kettle (n) _____

13. abruptly (adv) _____

14. disturb (v) _____

15. dreamy (adj) _____

Write on the line the correct list word to complete each sentence.

The rain stopped as __ as it had started.	1. _____
The loud siren began to __ those playing on the baseball field.	2. _____
They offered pizza as an __ for those who sold the most tickets.	3. _____
The professor is paid his __ every two weeks.	4. _____
The __ locks the doors at the end of each day.	5. _____
A __ in the stone at Mount Rushmore depicts the faces of four United States presidents.	6. _____
Please put the plastic into that __ to be recycled.	7. _____
Tim believed that if he worked hard, he would __.	8. _____
The __ of the park is not to feed the bears.	9. _____
My grandmother had a lime green __ she used to make tea.	10. _____

C Circle the correct word.

1. Which word is someone new?

    a)   novice   b)   kettle   c)   policy   d)   salary

2. Which is another word for "money"?

    a)   novice   b)   kettle   c)   policy   d)   salary

3. What word is the opposite of "normal"?

    a)   eccentric   b)   kettle   c)   policy   d)   carvings

4. Which of these words means "to talk"?

    a)   abruptly   b)   incentive   c)   blouse   d)   discuss

5. Which word could refer to doing well financially at a job?

    a)   dreamy   b)   disturbed   c)   kettle   d)   prosper

 D Circle two words which have either similar or opposite meanings. Write the letter S if they are similar, or O if they are opposite.

1. blouse   hat   shirt   shoes   _____

2. bow   bowling   bowl   container   _____

3. cot   kettle   pot   hot   _____

4. rule   rude   police   policy   _____

5. senses   incense   incentive   reason   _____

Optional: Use a thesaurus to find more synonyms and antonyms for the list words.

CROSSWORD PUZZLE Use the words from this lesson to complete the crossword puzzle.

ACROSS

1 person who takes care of something

6 something into which other things can be put

8 set of rules

10 succeed

13 bother

14 money paid for work done

15 beginner

DOWN

2 appearing to be daydreaming

3 not usual or normal

4 talk about

5 pot for boiling

7 suddenly

9 something meant to make a person work harder

11 an object or design made by cutting

12 woman's shirt

Vocabulary Lesson

23

A Write the dictionary definition for the specific part of speech (noun, verb, adjective, or adverb).

1. nation (n) _____

2. border (n) _____

3. shallow (adj) _____

4. commit (v) _____

5. contribution (n) _____

6. funds (n) _____

7. legal (adj) _____

8. plunder (v) _____

9. blame (v) _____

10. confer (v) _____

11. expert (n) _____

12. burden (n) _____

13. blunt (adj) _____

14. appease (v) _____

15. vision (n) _____

Write on the line the correct list word to complete each sentence.

The pope will __ with the bishops before the Mass.	1.
The Church asks that we make a __ of some of our income.	2.
Father asked the altar boys to __ to serving at a Sunday Mass.	3.
The stream was too __ for us to swim.	4.
The policeman said it is not __ to skate in the street.	5.
Jimmy did not have the __ to buy a new bike.	6.
The United States has always been one __ under God.	7.
The United States shares a __ with Canada in the north.	8.
After years of study, Thomas has become an __ in art history.	9.
My ___ was blurred by the pouring rain on my glasses.	10.

Jesus, Mary, Joseph, I love You!

C   Circle the correct word.

1. Which word says something a good person would not do?

    a)   vision   b)   nation   c)   plunder   d)   expert

2. Which word means to accuse someone?

    a)   blame   b)   appease   c)   blunt   d)   committed

3. Which word could you use to mean a heavy thing?

    a)   nation   b)   legal   c)   shallow   d)   burden

4. Which word means a person with great knowledge?

    a)   vision   b)   expert   c)   blunt   d)   burden

5. Which word would you use when writing about money?

    a)   funds   b)   border   c)   vision   d)   legal

D   Circle two words which have either similar or opposite meanings. Write the letter S if they are similar, or O if they are opposite.

1. nation   king   county   country   _____

2. keep   deep   shallow   seep   _____

3. blunder   sharp   bland   blunt   _____

4. legal   border   label   edge   _____

5. confer   plunder   burden   discuss   _____

Optional: Use a thesaurus to find more synonyms and antonyms for the list words.

Use the words from this lesson to complete the crossword puzzle.

ACROSS

6 donation
7 find fault with
8 available money
10 make calm
12 country
13 rob
14 person with special knowledge
of a subject

DOWN

1 dull
2 allowed by law
3 compare views
4 sight
5 to bind oneself to do something
7 a heavy or difficult load
9 not deep
11 boundary

Vocabulary Lesson

24

A Write the dictionary definition for the specific part of speech (noun, verb, adjective, or adverb).

1. museum (n) _____

2. department (n) _____

3. watertight (adj) _____

4. filter (v) _____

5. moisture (n) _____

6. valve (n) _____

7. bureau (n) _____

8. carve (v) _____

9. canyon (n) _____

10. sanctify (v) _____

11. truce (n) _____

12. surround (v) _____

13. capital (n) _____

14. update (v) _____

15. vestment (n) _____

B Write on the line the correct list word to complete each sentence.

Kevin wants to __ his computer with the new computer program.	1.
The fishermen made sure that the boat was __ before they sailed.	2.
In Arizona, we rode a donkey through a small __.	3.
Joseph will __ a wooden crucifix for the married couple.	4.
Graces from God __ us.	5.
After many months of fighting, the two sides agreed to a __.	6.
The crowd began to __ Jesus as He healed the sick.	7.
The boys put their shirts in the old __ in their room.	8.
Dad turned off the water __ because the faucet was leaking.	9.
For a field trip, Mom took us to a science __.	10.

Jesus, Mary, Joseph, I love You!

C Circle the correct word.

1. Which is something you could do with wood?

   a) surround   b) filter   c) carve   d) update

2. Which word means to "make holy"?

   a) gleamed   b) truce   c) sanctify   d) surround

3. What word is the opposite of "dryness"?

   a) bureau   b) valve   c) capital   d) moisture

4. Which word means a device that blocks a liquid in a pipe?

   a) filtered   b) valve   c) carved   d) update

5. Which word refers to where people keep clothes?

   a) bureau   b) valve   c) canyon   d) truce

D Circle two words which have either similar or opposite meanings. Write the letter S if they are similar, or O if they are opposite.

1. vestment   surround   garment   bureau   _____

2. true   truce   warn   war   _____

3. enter   surround   enhance   encircle   _____

4. capital   man   money   many   _____

5. valley   valve   canyon   tapped   _____

Optional: Use a thesaurus to find more synonyms and antonyms for the list words.

Use the words from this lesson to complete the crossword puzzle.

ACROSS

3 accumulated wealth from money or property
7 give the latest information
10 building where objects of interest are displayed
11 make holy
12 to pass through something
13 agreement to stop fighting
14 chest of drawers

DOWN

1 device that blocks a flow
2 special division of an organization
4 made to keep water out
5 cut with care
6 deep valley
8 enclose on all sides
9 outer garment
10 dampness

Vocabulary 4 for Young Catholics
Glossary

abbot – head of an abbey
abruptly – suddenly
accommodate – provide with a place to stay
acquire – gain
adjustable – able to be changed
admire – think very highly of
advertise – announce publicly
advice – suggestions
advise – give suggestions
alert – watchful
amusing – entertaining
ancient – very old
angle – two lines meeting at a point
annoying – irritating
annual – happening once a year
appease – make calm
approach – come near
arrange – put in order
assemble – gather
assist – help
assistant – helper
associate – person with whom one works
attempt – try to do
autumn – season between summer and winter
avert – turn away
banish – force to leave
banquet – formal dinner
barrier – something that blocks the way
batter – mixture of flour and liquid for cooking
blame – find fault with
blouse – woman's shirt
blunt – dull
board – to get on as onto a ship or plane
border – boundary
branch – grows out from the trunk of a tree
brief – short; not long
brilliant – very bright
burden – something heavy or hard to carry
bureau – chest of drawers
business – the activity of making, buying, and selling

buzzard – large bird of prey
canoe – long narrow boat
canyon – deep valley
capable – able to accomplish something
capital – accumulated wealth from money or property
capital – location of a government in a country or state as capital city
carcass – dead body of an animal
carve – cut with care
carving – an object or design made by cutting
cathedral – main church of a diocese
century – one hundred years
ceramic – made of baked clay
chance – opportunity
chapel – small church
charity – love
chef – cook
chief – most important
classic – judged to be of timeless quality among the best of its kind
cleric – member of the clergy
clumsy – lacking skill in movement; not graceful
coastline – boundary between land and ocean
colorful – having bright colors
column – long row
commit – to bind oneself to do something
companion – person who goes with another
complaint – expression of dissatisfaction
conduct – personal behavior
confection – fancy sweet food
confer – compare views
confuse – make uncertain; to mix up
congregation – assembly of persons
conquer – overcome
consider – think over carefully
construction – the process of building
container – something into which other things can be put
continent – great division of land on the globe
contribution – donation

convert – change a person's beliefs
convict – prove guilty
correctly – rightly
courtyard – enclosed space next to a building
creative – imaginative
creep – to move slowly or quietly
crew – group of people working together
crouch – stoop or bend low
crozier – bishop's staff
crucial – very important
cruise – pleasure trip on a ship
custodian – person who takes care of something
daily – every day
damage – cause harm
dance – series of movements in time to music
debt – something owed
decade – period of ten years
delighted – pleased
demonstrate – show clearly
depart – leave
department – special division of an organization
dependable – reliable
deplete – reduce in amount by using up
desert – leave a duty or person
desire – want
destination – goal of a journey
detail – small part of something larger
deter – prevent from acting
determine – come to a decision
dictionary – book giving the meaning of words
digestion – the body's process of changing (breaking up) food
diocese – area under the authority of a bishop
disagree – differ in opinion
discipline – training that corrects or strengthens
discover – find out
discuss – talk about
disguise – hide
distance – how far apart two things are
distant – far away
disturb – bother
donate – give away
dreamy – appearing to be daydreaming
eager – wanting very much
eccentric – not usual or normal

educational – having to do with learning
eerie – causing uneasiness and fear; strange
embrace – hug; clasp in the arms
embroider – decorate with needlework
empire – group of territories under one ruler
encircle – surround
encouraging – giving confidence
entertainment – amusement
equipment – tools
erect – put up; build
escape – get away
examine – look at carefully
example – model to be imitated
exile – force someone to leave his own country
expedition – journey
expert – person with special knowledge of a subject
extend – stretch out
eyesight – vision
fabric – cloth
faint – not clear
fantastic – extremely good
farther – at a greater distance
fascinating – extremely interesting
feeble – lacking strength
festival – celebration
fictional – made–up
filter – to pass through something
fleet – swift
foolish – lacking good sense
form – to make
fowl – a bird; a hen or a rooster
frail – delicate
funds – available money
furious – very angry
future – coming after the present
garment – article of clothing
gasp – breathe in suddenly
gloomy – sad
gnaw – bite or chew upon
government – political rule
grasp – lay hold of with the mind; understand
gratitude – feeling of appreciation
guide – someone that shows the way
handful – small number

harass – annoy again and again

healthy – sound and well

hero – person of great courage

heroic – courageous

hold – interior of a ship below a deck

hopeful – having hope; expecting something to happen; being wishful

humorous – funny

hunt – a search

illustrate – explain or make clear by examples

imagine – to picture in the mind

immoral – wicked

impassable – impossible to cross

incentive – something meant to make a person work harder

inform – let a person know something

injure – cause harm

inquire – ask about

instruct – teach

intention – aim

interpreter – person who translates spoken words

inventor – person who thinks up or makes new things

issue – flow out

jagged – sharply uneven

journey – long trip

judge – form an opinion after careful consideration

kettle – pot for boiling

kingdom – country ruled by a king or queen

legal – allowed by law

liberate – set free

lonely – not often visited

"magazine – publication with stories, articles, and poems"

maroon – dark red

melody – pleasing arrangement of sounds

merchant – person who buys and sells goods

Messiah – Deliverer of God's Chosen People

mission – task or job

miter – bishop's cap

modernize – to make suitable for the present time

moisture – dampness; slight wetness

monastery – place where monks live

moral – virtuous; good

mountain – mass of land higher than a hill

museum – building where objects of interest are displayed

nation – country

nave – central part of a church

navigate – steer a course

nearer – closer

novice – beginner

objective – goal

observe – watch; pay attention to

obvious – easily understood

occasion – special event

occupant – one who stays or lives in a place (a room or a building)

occupy – live in as a tenant

offer – to present

operate – work in a proper way

ordain – give Holy Orders

orderly – tidy

overlook – fail to see

owner – person who owns or possesses something

pagan – connected with a person who does not know about God

panel – rectangular section above or below the surrounding area: a panel on a door

paragraph – group of sentences on one topic

parish – part of a diocese under authority of a priest

parrot – brightly colored bird

passion – strong emotion

pastry – sweet baked good

patron – guardian or protector

peculiar – odd; different from the usual

peppermint – plant used in flavoring

perhaps – maybe

perilous – dangerous

persecution – continual cruel treatment

phony – not real or genuine

pilot – person who flies a plane

plantation – large area of land where crops are grown

platform – raised floor

platter – large plate

plot – plan secretly

plunder – rob

plush – soft and thick
policy – a set of rules
port – place for ships and boats
possible – able to be done
precious – valuable
predict – foretell
present – being here and not elsewhere
pretend – make believe
process – series of actions leading to a result
professor – teacher
property – something that is owned
prophet – person who declares a message from God
prosper – succeed
protect – to keep from being harmed
provide – give what is needed
puff – blow in short gusts
pulpit – raised platform for preaching
purchase – buy
pursue – chase
puzzle – mystery
rations – food
reasonable – sensible
recite – repeat from memory
reflect – give back an image
regret – be sorry
rehearse – practice
release – set free
religious – devoted to God
remove – get rid of
repeat – tell again
repent – be sorry for having sinned
request – ask for something
reside – dwell
respond – answer; reply
restore – return to good condition
resume – begin again
revive – bring back into use
revolve – rotate
risky – dangerous
roam – wander
royal – relating to a king or queen
salary – money paid for work done
sanctify – make holy
satisfy – make someone content (pleased)
scene – view that resembles a picture

scheme – form a secret plan
schooner – ship with two masts
scoundrel – wicked person
scramble – move or climb quickly
sculptor – person who makes statues
scurry – move quickly
section – a part separated or cut off
seize – take by force
separate – set apart
severely – harshly
shallow – not deep
shore – land along the edge of water
sight – something seen
skilled – having ability
slavery – bondage
slower – moving with less speed
solemn – serious and dignified
specimen – example
splendid – impressive in beauty
spring – season between winter and summer
startle – frighten suddenly but slightly
steady – showing little change
straight – in a direct manner, course, or line
strive – try hard
structure – something built in a definite way
struggle – make a great effort to do something
stubborn – refusing to change
stumble – trip
support – assist
surround – enclose on all sides; encircle
survive – remain alive
tabernacle – structure that contains the Holy Eucharist
talent – special ability
tempest – strong wind often with much rain, hail, or snow
tend – take care of
terrified – afraid
theater – where plays are presented
toil – work hard
tour – travel from place to place
trade – one's work or occupation
trample – crush under the feet
transform – change completely
trellis – lattice frame
truce – agreement to stop fighting

understand – get the meaning of

update – give the latest information

valley – low land between mountains

valuable – of great worth

valve – device that blocks a flow

vessel – ship

vestment – outer garment

vicious – violent and cruel

vision – sight

vivid – very bright

vocabulary – list of words

vocation – calling; occupation

vow – make a solemn promise

voyage – long journey by water

wander – walk without a purpose

wardrobe – the clothes a person owns

warehouse – building for storing goods

warmth – gentle heat

watertight – made to keep water out

wealthy – rich

weep – cry

welfare – well–being

wondrous – marvelous

wound – injury

yearn – desire something very much